Usborne

Illustrated Atlas of
Britain & Ireland

Struan Reid & Megan Cullis

Illustrated by
Adam Larkum

Designed by
Emily Barden & Katie Webb

Cartographer
Jenny Slater

Usborne Quicklinks

To explore famous sites of Britain and Ireland visit Usborne Quicklinks. There you'll find links to websites with video tours, fun facts and activities to find out more about some of the places in this book. Go to **www.usborne.com/quicklinks** and type in the keywords 'Britain and Ireland'.

Please read our online safety guidelines at the Usborne Quicklinks.
Children should be supe

D1355210

Contents

The British Isles

The British Isles consist of two separate countries — the United Kingdom and the Republic of Ireland.

Altogether they're made up of more than 6,000 islands, of which the largest is Great Britain.

The island of Great Britain is made up of England, Scotland and Wales.

The island of Ireland consists of Northern Ireland, which is part of the United Kingdom, and the Republic of Ireland.

Key

These are some of the features to look for on the maps in this book.

- ■ CAPITAL CITIES
- ● TOWNS & CITIES
- MOUNTAINS
- RIVERS
- COUNTRY BOUNDARY
- COUNTY OR REGIONAL BOUNDARIES

Shetland Islands

Orkney Islands

Outer Hebrides

Inner Hebrides

NORTHERN SCOTLAND

GLASGOW

EDINBURGH

SOUTHERN SCOTLAND

IRELAND

NORTHERN IRELAND

BELFAST

ATLANTIC OCEAN

REPUBLIC OF IRELAND

DUBLIN

Isle of Man

NORTH WEST

NORTH EAST

NORTH SEA

YORK

Anglesey

MANCHESTER

LIVERPOOL

GREAT BRITAIN

IRISH SEA

WALES

THE MIDLANDS

EAST OF ENGLAND

CAMBRIDGE

CARDIFF

BRISTOL

OXFORD

BATH

LONDON

SOUTH WEST

SOUTH EAST

Isles of Scilly

Isle of Wight

ENGLISH CHANNEL

South West

Thomas Hardy
Novelist and poet
Born near Dorchester, Dorset
1840-1928

"...that wild weird western shore..."

This is a description of the Cornish coast, from Thomas Hardy's poem *Beeny Cliff*.

1 The small fishing town of **St Ives** has attracted artists since the 19th century — from painter J. M. W. Turner to sculptor Barbara Hepworth. It's now full of galleries, including the Tate St Ives and the Barbara Hepworth Museum.

Fewer than 30 people live on the windswept island of **Lundy** — but it's home to hundreds of puffins and other birds.

Bristol Channel

Lundy

Exmoor National Park

BARNSTAPLE

Devonshire cream tea

The Tarka Line

KERNOW A'GAS DYNERGH
WELCOME TO CORNWALL

This road sign is written in both Cornish and English. 'Kernow' is Cornish for Cornwall.

2 According to legend, **King Arthur** ruled Britain with his Knights of the Round Table during the late 5th century. Some historians think he was a real person — born in Tintagel Castle, Cornwall.

King Arthur

Cawl! Cawl!

Cornish chough

BEENY
TINTAGEL

② *Cornish pasty*

River Tamar

BODMIN

Dartmoor National Park

EXETE

TORQUA

Land's End is the most westerly point of mainland Britain.

① ST IVES

NEWQUAY

Eden Project

PLYMOUTH

CORNWALL

TRURO

Truro Cathedral

Isles of Scilly

Land's End

In the clear waters around the **Isles of Scilly**, people can swim with wild seals.

During the 17th century, the remote rocky inlets around Cornwall's coast made it easy for **smugglers** to sneak goods, such as tea and silks, ashore.

In 1588, the English navy set sail from Plymouth to defeat the **Spanish Armada** — a fleet of ships sent from Spain to invade England.

In August every year, hundreds of hot air balloons fill the skies during Bristol's International Balloon Fiesta.

SS *Great Britain* was designed by Isambard Kingdom Brunel and built in Bristol. In 1845 it became the first iron steamship to cross the Atlantic Ocean.

Horses thunder across Cheltenham Racecourse during the Cheltenham Gold Cup.

Gloucester Cathedral

River Severn

CHELTENHAM
● **GLOUCESTER**

③

Discover more about Bristol on page 32.

A Gloucestershire Old Spot pig

Oink!

GLOUCESTERSHIRE

BRISTOL ●

There's more about Bath on page 37.

⑤
● **BATH**

Severn Estuary

WILTSHIRE

GLASTONBURY

Festival-goers travel from all over the world to listen to musicians at Glastonbury Festival.

White horse figure, carved into the hillside

④
SALISBURY ●

Cheddar Gorge

TAUNTON ●

Scrumpy is a type of cider made in the South West.

SOMERSET

DEVON

Salisbury Cathedral has the tallest church spire in Britain.

DORSET

DORCHESTER
POOLE ●

● **LYME REGIS**

⑥

Corfe Castle

● **BOURNEMOUTH**

Portland Bill

Arthur Conan Doyle set his detective novel, The Hound of the Baskervilles, in Dartmoor National Park.

Portland Bill Lighthouse, built in 1906, guides ships across the English Channel.

ENGLISH CHANNEL

Agatha Christie
Novelist and playwright
Born in Torquay, Devon
1890-1976

Walter Raleigh
Soldier and explorer
Born near Torquay, Devon
1552-1618

Mary Anning
Fossil collector
Born in Lyme Regis, Dorset
1799-1847

3 Once a year, people in Gloucestershire roll a cheese down a hill in the Cooper's Hill Cheese Rolling Race.

4 **Stonehenge** is a huge stone monument that's over 4,000 years old. It's thought to be an ancient ceremonial site.

5 The city of **Bath** is named after its ancient Roman baths — bathing pools supplied by natural hot springs.

6 Fossils of prehistoric animals, up to 185 million years old, have been found on the **Jurassic Coast** — a stretch of coastline between Dorset and East Devon.

South East

1 Founded in around 1096, the **University of Oxford** is one of the oldest universities in the world.

2 **Hampton Court Palace** sits on the banks of the River Thames. King Henry VIII of England (1491-1547) was the first monarch to live there.

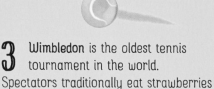

3 **Wimbledon** is the oldest tennis tournament in the world. Spectators traditionally eat strawberries and cream between matches.

Ooooh!

4 The restless ghosts of King George III and Queen Elizabeth I are said to haunt **Windsor Castle**.

Aaaah!

5 On the **Isle of Wight**, you can see the fossilized footprints of dinosaurs that roamed the Earth millions of years ago.

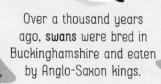

Over a thousand years ago, **swans** were bred in Buckinghamshire and eaten by Anglo-Saxon kings.

MILTON KEYNES

During the Second World War, codebreakers worked at **Bletchley Park** near Milton Keynes, decoding secret messages.

Blenheim Palace is the birthplace of British prime minister Winston Churchill (1874-1965).

Rowers go head-to-head at the **Henley Regatta**, a race on the Thames.

OXFORDSHIRE

1 OXFORD

BUCKINGHAMSHIRE

Find out more about Oxford on page 34.

HIGH WYCOMBE

River Thames

READING

Ascot races

4 ASCOT

Highclere Castle

BERKSHIRE

Royal Military Academy, Sandhurst

SURREY

WOKING

BASINGSTOKE

HAMPSHIRE

Winchester Cathedral choir

Hikers walk along the South Downs Way – a path that crosses the South Downs National Park.

WINCHESTER

At 2,000 years old, the **Kingley Vale yew trees** are some of the oldest living things in Britain.

EMBLEY

SOUTHAMPTON

New Forest National Park

West Quay Centre

South Downs National Park

WEST SUSSEX

PORTSMOUTH

BOGNOR REGIS

The Solent

COWES

5 NEWPORT

Isle of Wight

During the International Birdman competition, human 'birdmen' jump off Bognor Regis Pier in fancy dress.

Chalk columns, called The Needles

Florence Nightingale
Nurse and social reformer
Brought up at Embley, Hampshire
1820-1910

Standing 309.6m (1,016ft) high, **The Shard** is Britain's tallest building.

Charles Dickens
Writer
Born in Portsmouth, Hampshire
1812-1870

Malorie Blackman
Writer
Born in London
1962

There's more on London on pages 24-25.

..."The White Cliffs of Dover"...

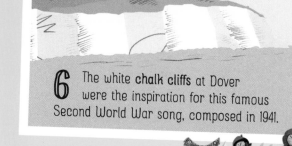

6 The white **chalk cliffs** at Dover were the inspiration for this famous Second World War song, composed in 1941.

7 Written by Geoffrey Chaucer more than 600 years ago, *The Canterbury Tales* tell the story of a group of pilgrims on the way from London to Canterbury Cathedral. Chaucer wrote the tales in an early form of English.

"And specially, from every shires ende of Engelond, to Caunterbury they wende..."
From Chaucer's General Prologue to *The Canterbury Tales*

LONDON

River Thames

GREATER LONDON

2 3

Around 700 planes land and take off from **Gatwick Airport**, near Crawley, every day.

CRAWLEY

River Medway

An **oast house**, where hops are dried to make beer

GILLINGHAM

Thrill-seekers enjoy rides at the Dreamland theme park in Margate. Wheee!

MARGATE

CANTERBURY *River Stour* **7**

Canterbury Cathedral

ENGLISH CHANNEL

Dover Castle **DOVER** **6**

FOLKESTONE

A rail tunnel, called the **Channel Tunnel**, runs for 37.8km (23.5 miles) underwater, connecting England to France.

KENT

The **Ashdown Forest** is the setting for the children's book *Winnie-the-Pooh*, by A. A. Milne.

Banoffee pie was invented in East Sussex.

EAST SUSSEX

Dungeness lighthouse

HASTINGS

BRIGHTON

EASTBOURNE

Brighton Pier

At the **Battle of Hastings** in 1066, an English army was defeated by the Normans from France. King Harold of England is said to have been killed by an arrow through his eye.

Cap Gris-Nez

Trained swimmers can swim all 32km (21 miles) across the English Channel, from Dover, England to Cap Gris-Nez, France.

ENGLISH CHANNEL

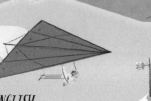

East of England

"I am myself a Norfolk man and glory in being so!"

From a speech Nelson made in 1800

1 For thousands of years the Fens was a vast area of bogs and marshland. In the 17th century it was drained of water and is now fertile farmland.

2 In 1216, King John was on his way from King's Lynn to Lincoln when he attempted to cross The Wash. Legend has it that the waters swept away his baggage cart with the Crown Jewels inside.

Edith Cavell
Nurse
Born near Norwich, Norfolk
1865-1915

While working as a nurse in Belgium during the First World War, Edith Cavell was arrested and executed by German forces.

Cromer crabs are a tasty speciality of Norfolk.

Horatio Nelson
Vice Admiral and Royal Navy commander
Born in Burnham Thorpe, Norfolk
1758-1805

King's Lynn was once a very important port. During the Middle Ages, fish was imported there from Scandinavia, timber from the Baltics and wine from France.

Blakeney Point

Every year, from November to January, hundreds of **seals** gather on the beaches at Blakeney Point to give birth to their pups.

SHERINGHAM

HOLT

The Broads National Park

NORWICH

Sainsbury Centre for Visual Arts

Thetford Forest

GREAT YARMOUTH

LOWESTOFT

Southwold beach huts

SOUTHWOLD

• BURNHAM THORPE

Visitors can catch a ride on a steam train on the **Poppy Line**, between Sheringham and Holt.

NORFOLK

• KING'S LYNN

According to legend, a ghostly black dog called **Black Shuck** roams the Fens.

Grrr!

Sugar beet is grown on farms in Suffolk.

River Great Ouse

The Wash **2**

Oliver Cromwell
Military and political leader
Born in Huntingdon, Cambridgeshire
1599-1658

Marsh harrier

• PETERBOROUGH

CAMBRIDGESHIRE

You can see the tomb of Catherine of Aragon, first wife of King Henry VIII, in Peterborough Cathedral.

Inside Ely Cathedral

ELY

Airlander 10, an airship and the world's largest aircraft, is being developed near Bedford.

HUNTINGDON

There's more about Cambridge on page 35.

④

CAMBRIDGE
Cambridge University was founded in 1209.

River Cam

NEWMARKET

③

SAFFRON WALDEN

Saffron Walden takes its name from the **saffron crocus flowers** that were once grown here.

BEDFORDSHIRE

BEDFORD *River Great Ouse*

LUTON

Nadiya Hussain
Chef, author and television presenter
Born in Luton, Bedfordshire
1984

Luton International Airport is one of England's busiest airports.

HERTFORDSHIRE

WATFORD

Nicholas Breakspear
Elected Pope as Adrian IV
Born near Watford, Hertfordshire
1100–1159

3 All kinds of aircraft zoom through the skies during the Duxford air shows, from vintage biplanes to helicopters.

4 Punting on the River Cam is popular during summer months. A punt is a flat-bottomed boat, and punters use a wooden pole to push against the river bed and move the punt along.

BURY ST EDMUNDS

Ickworth House

SUFFOLK

⑥

During the 15th century, Lavenham was one of the richest towns in England. Merchants came here to buy and sell wool.

LAVENHAM

SUDBURY

COLCHESTER

Colchester Castle

Colchester was the **capital of Britain** in Roman times, about 2,000 years ago. It's the oldest recorded town in England.

ESSEX

⑤

CHELMSFORD

In 1899, Guglielmo Marconi opened the world's first **wireless radio factory** in Chelmsford.

BASILDON

SOUTHEND-ON-SEA

At 2.16km (1.34 miles) long, **Southend Pier** is the longest pleasure pier in the world.

FELIXSTOWE

Felixstowe Port is Britain's busiest container port.

IPSWICH

NORTH SEA

Thomas Gainsborough
Portrait and landscape painter
Born in Sudbury, Suffolk
1727–1788

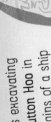

6 In 1939, archaeologists excavating an earth mound at **Sutton Hoo** in Suffolk discovered the remains of a ship packed with treasures. Once owned by an Anglo-Saxon king 1,400 years ago, these treasures can now be seen in the British Museum in London.

Helmet and gold buckle from Sutton Hoo

5 During the 1730s, Epping Forest was terrorized by a gang of deer thieves known as the **Essex Gang**. One member, named Dick Turpin, was eventually caught and executed, and his exploits have since become famous.

The Midlands

Josiah Wedgwood
Potter
Born in Burslem,
Staffordshire
1730-1795

Barn owl

The Peak District National Park opened as Britain's first national park in 1951.

Peak District National Park

BUXTON

Chatsworth House is a magnificent stately home just inside the Peak District.

1 According to legend, an outlaw named Robin Hood operated from Sherwood Forest in Nottinghamshire. He and his band of 'Merry Men' robbed the rich to help the poor, pursued by the 'wicked' Sheriff of Nottingham.

You can see bottle kilns in the Potteries, dating from the 18th and 19th centuries.

BURSLEM

DERBYSHIRE

DERBY

River Trent

The three spires of Lichfield Cathedral are known as 'The Three Sisters'.

2

Shropshire is famous for its **black and white houses**.

Iron Bridge

STAFFORDSHIRE

5 LICHFIELD

2 The National Memorial Arboretum is the United Kingdom's national site of remembrance. Dotted around the woodland landscape are more than 300 memorials.

SHREWSBURY

TELFORD

SHROPSHIRE

Much of Britain's **car industry** is based in the West Midlands.

Modern architecture in Birmingham, one of England's largest cities

BIRMINGHAM

WEST MIDLANDS

6

COVENTRY

Warwick Castle

WARWI[CK]

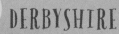

3 Hereford Cathedral is home to one of the world's oldest libraries, and a famous world map called the *Mappa Mundi*, dating from about 1300.

Hereford cattle were first bred in Herefordshire in the early 19th century. They are now found all around the world.

WORCESTERSHIRE

WARWICKSHIRE

River Severn

WORCESTER

7 STRATFORD-UPON-AVON

HEREFORDSHIRE

3

HEREFORD

Cricket is played near the cathedral in Worcester.

Lenny Henry
Actor and writer
Born near Birmingham
1958

River Wye

Herefordshire cider apple orchards

"Friendship is Love without his wings!"

Taken from Byron's poem *L'amitie est L'amour sans Ailes*

Wind turbines

Newstead Abbey

Lord Byron
Poet
Lived at Newstead Abbey,
Nottinghamshire
1788-1824

NORTH SEA

LINCOLN
The Lincoln Imp is a famous carving inside Lincoln Cathedral.

Lincolnshire Wolds

Skegness is a popular seaside resort.

SKEGNESS

1

TINGHAM

NOTTINGHAMSHIRE

LINCOLNSHIRE

WOOLSTHORPE

The Wash

MELTON MOWBRAY
Melton Mowbray is famous for its **pork pies.**

SHIRE

4 **LEICESTER**

RUTLAND

The Curve Theatre

FOTHERINGHAY

Mary, Queen of Scots was executed at Fotheringhay Castle in 1587.

6 In the mid-11th century, the legendary **Lady Godiva,** wife of the Earl of Mercia, is supposed to have ridden naked through Coventry in protest at her husband's severe taxes.

NORTHAMPTONSHIRE

NORTHAMPTON

Northampton is famous for its **shoe industry** and leatherworking.

4 In 2012, the skeleton of **King Richard III** was discovered under a car park in Leicester and was reburied in Leicester Cathedral.

Isaac Newton
Scientist and author
Born in Woolsthorpe,
Lincolnshire
1643-1727

5 In 2009, the **Staffordshire Hoard** was discovered by a metal detectorist near Lichfield in Staffordshire. It is the largest collection of Anglo-Saxon gold and silver ever found.

7 The **Royal Shakespeare Company** is based at William Shakespeare's birthplace of Stratford-upon-Avon. It puts on around 20 productions a year.

"This blessed plot, this earth, this realm, this England."

From *Richard II*, Act 2 Scene 1

William Shakespeare
Playwright and poet
Born in Stratford-upon-Avon,
Warwickshire
1564-1616

North West

2 Often described as 'the backbone of England', the **Pennines** are a range of mountains and hills that separates North West and North East England. The area includes some of the most scenic parts of Britain.

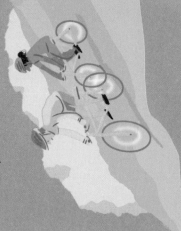

Famous for her stories about **Peter Rabbit** and other animals, Beatrix Potter lived for much of her life in the Lake District.

Beatrix Potter
Writer, illustrator, conservationist
Born in London
1866–1943

William Wordsworth
Poet
Born in Cockermouth, Cumbria
1770–1850

"I wandered lonely as a cloud
That floats on high o'er vales and hills,
When all at once I saw a crowd,
A host, of golden daffodils."

From *I Wandered Lonely as a Cloud*, a poem written by Wordsworth after a walk in the Lake District

David Yip
Actor and playwright
Born in Liverpool
1951

For over 150 years, Barrow-in-Furness has been a centre of ship- and submarine-building.

BIRDOSWALD ● 1

At Penrith you can see a group of ancient tombstones known as The Giant's Grave.

Lowther Castle

Pennines

2

Yorkshire Dales National Park

Lonk sheep

● KENDAL

Whinchat

CARLISLE ●

PENRITH ●

Dalemain Marmalade Festival

Lake Windermere

CUMBRIA

Kendal mint cake

Keswick Pencil Museum

KESWICK ●

Lake District

3

Scafell Pike

BARROW-IN-FURNESS

Cumberland sausage

Solway Firth

COCKERMOUTH ●

WORKINGTON ●

WHITEHAVEN ●

St Bees Head

IRISH SEA

Black guillemot

The Lady Isabella waterwheel is the largest working waterwheel in the world.

The three-legged triskelion symbol has been used as the badge of the Isle of Man since the 13th century.

The Isle of Man TT motorcycle races have been held every May and June since 1907. They are one of the world's most dangerous racing events.

The Southport 24-hour Race is an endurance race for dinghies held every September.

Isle of Man

● DOUGLAS

● FLEETWOOD

● BLACKPOOL

● LYTHAM ST ANNES

● SOUTHPORT

● LANCASTER

Lytham St Annes has hosted the open championship golf tournament 11 times.

④

● CLITHEROE
The world's first jet engine was developed at Clitheroe during the early 1940s.

The Singing Ringing Tree sculpture stands above Burnley.

● BURNLEY

● BLACKBURN

Bowland Wild Boar Park

LANCASHIRE

Discover more about Manchester on page 30.

The waterfront area of Salford Quays in Manchester contains The Lowry arts complex.

● MANCHESTER

GREATER MANCHESTER

For 400 years, Stockport was an important town for hat-making.

● STOCKPORT

Peak District National Park

CHESHIRE

Cheshire Cheese

Lancashire Hotpot

There's more about Liverpool on page 33.

⑥

● LIVERPOOL

⑤

MERSEYSIDE

● BIRKENHEAD

Liverpool Bay

River Mersey

● CREWE

● CHESTER
At Chester you can see the remains of Britain's largest Roman amphitheatre.

Minke whale

3 A mountainous area famous for its lakes and forests. The Lake District contains Scafell Pike, the highest mountain in England.

During the 1950s and 60s, Donald Campbell set the world water speed record, racing *Bluebird* in the Lake District.

4 The Roman Ribchester Helmet was found at Ribchester in 1796. You can now see it in the British Museum in London.

5 Formed in Liverpool in 1960, **The Beatles** was one of the world's most famous rock bands and one of the most influential music bands in history. The group disbanded in 1970.

Bluebird

6 Held at Aintree Racecourse in Liverpool and first run in 1839. The Grand National is one of the most famous horse races in the world.

THE BEATLES

North East

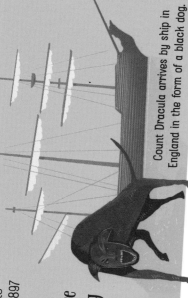

1 Author **Bram Stoker** is thought to have gained inspiration for his 1897 story *Dracula* after a visit to Whitby.

"... the very instant the shore was touched, an immense dog sprang up on the deck from below ... and jumped from the bow to the sand."

Count Dracula arrives by ship in England in the form of a black dog.

Grace Darling
Lighthouse keeper
Born in Bamburgh,
Northumberland
1815-1842

In 1838, Grace and her father rescued the survivors of a paddlesteamer wrecked on the Farne Islands.

2 The Angel of the North is an enormous steel sculpture, 20m (66ft) tall with a wingspan of 54m (177ft).

James Cook
Explorer and Royal Navy captain
Born near Middlesbrough,
North Yorkshire
1728-1779

NORTH SEA

The Holy Island of Lindisfarne was an important early Christian site.

Thousands of puffins and other birds live on the Farne Islands.

Minke whales

Gateshead Millennium Bridge near Newcastle

There's a busy ferry route between Newcastle and Amsterdam in the Netherlands.

Royal Border Bridge

Berwick-upon-Tweed, the northernmost town in England, was fought over for centuries by the English and Scots.

Alnwick Castle is a magnificent 1,000 year-old castle and private home.

River Tweed

BERWICK-UPON-TWEED

Lindisfarne

Farne Islands

• **BAMBURGH**

• **ALNWICK**

Northumberland National Park

Ashington was once an important coal mining area, where today you can visit a colliery museum.

• **ASHINGTON**

NORTHUMBERLAND

Hadrian's Wall

Barn owl

Chevoit Hills

Towering over the River Wear, Durham Cathedral is one of the most impressive sites in England.

River Tyne

NEWCASTLE-UPON-TYNE

TYNE & WEAR

• **SUNDERLAND**

② ③

• **DURHAM**

• **HARTLEPOOL**

WHITBY ①
Robin Hood's Bay

Built in 1669, the Chalk Tower is England's oldest surviving lighthouse.

Flamborough Head

Bridlington Bay

Burton Constable Hall is one of Yorkshire's finest stately homes.

Humber Estuary

The Tees Transporter Bridge at Middlesbrough carries people and vehicles across the River Tees.

SCARBOROUGH

You can take a steam train around the North York Moors.

EAST YORKSHIRE

KINGSTON UPON HULL

When it opened in 1981, the **Humber Bridge** was the world's longest single-span suspension bridge.

Once known as Steel City, Sheffield was one of the main places of steel production. Today, it is one of England's largest cities, with all kinds of businesses.

NORTH YORKSHIRE

North York Moors National Park

Yorkshire pudding

Near Ripon, you can visit the majestic ruins of Fountains Abbey.

River Swale

Yorkshire Wolds

River Ouse

You can find out more about York on page 36.

YORK

An important town in the 19th-century Industrial Revolution, Barnsley has a tradition of brass band music.

Skipton is a market town with a medieval castle. **HARROGATE**

RIPON

Otter

Yorkshire Dales National Park

SKIPTON

WEST YORKSHIRE

River Aire

LEEDS ④

BRADFORD

HUDDERSFIELD

BARNSLEY

DONCASTER

SOUTH YORKSHIRE

SHEFFIELD

Huddersfield is a large market town and the birthplace of Rugby League.

4 The Royal Armouries Museum in Leeds houses the national collection of arms and armour, from all periods and from across the world. Visitors can also see re-enactments of jousting tournaments.

Nicola Adams
Professional boxer and Olympic gold medallist
Born in Leeds, West Yorkshire
1982

Jessica Ennis-Hill
Athlete and Olympic gold medallist
Born in Sheffield, South Yorkshire
1986

The Brontë sisters
Born near Bradford, Charlotte (1816-55), Emily (1818-48) and Anne (1820-49) are famous all over the world for their writings, including *Jane Eyre* and *Wuthering Heights*.

3 Beamish Museum tells the story of life in North East England from the early 19th century through to the mid-20th century.

Wales

1 Owain Glyndŵr (1359-1415) was the last Welshman to hold the title Prince of Wales. He was based in the north east of Wales from where he led a rebellion against English rule.

2 For more than 100 years, a small steam train has been carrying tourists up to the top of **Mount Snowdon**, the highest mountain in Wales.

Red kite

The Chirk Aqueduct carries the Llangollen Canal over the Wales–England border.

WREXHAM

Dee Estuary

IRISH SEA

PRESTATYN

1

CLWYD

Welsh cakes are small, spiced currant cakes eaten all over Wales.

River Dee

With its treasures and famous gardens, Powis Castle towers over the surrounding landscape.

WELSHPOOL

River Severn

Conwy Castle

Snowdonia National Park

Welsh pony

Mount Snowdon

2

GWYNEDD

PORTMEIRION

Portmeirion is a miniature village in the Italian style, full of brightly painted houses.

Beaumaris Castle

Anglesey

HOLYHEAD

Holyhead is the largest town on Anglesey and has a busy port, with ferries to Dublin.

Bardsey Island

IRISH SEA

Bardsey Island is home to Manx shearwaters and seals.

"Years and years ago, when I was a boy, when there were wolves in Wales, and birds the colour of red flannel petticoats whished past the harp-shaped hills..."

From *A Child's Christmas in Wales*

Dylan Thomas
Poet and writer
Born in Swansea,
West Glamorgan
1914-1953

Grace Coddington
Model and magazine
creative director
Born in Anglesey
1941

With over 20 bookshops, Hay-on-Wye is known as the 'town of books'. The **Hay Festival** of literature is held here every year.

You can take a **steam train** from Aberystwyth through the beautiful Rheidol Vale.

At Aberystwyth there's a famous university and the National Library of Wales.

You can see bottlenose dolphins swimming in Cardigan Bay.

Cardigan Bay

River Wye

POWYS ③

HAY-ON-WYE

Horse racing has been held at Chepstow since 1926.

GWENT

CHEPSTOW

⑤

NEWPORT

CAERPHILLY

Severn Estuary

Caerphilly is famous for its cheese.

Brecon Beacons National Park

With its spectacular landscapes, the Brecon Beacons National Park was established in 1957.

Discover more about Cardiff on page 27.

CARDIFF

SOUTH GLAMORGAN

Bristol Channel

5 Two road bridges cross the Severn Estuary, linking Wales and England.

River Tywi

LLANDOVERY

River Teifi

The 17th-century Cardigan Bridge crosses the River Teifi.

DYFED

CARDIGAN

Dinas Head

Pembrokeshire Coast National Park

National Botanic Garden of Wales

CARMARTHEN

WEST GLAMORGAN

PORT TALBOT

④

MID GLAMORGAN

SWANSEA

Swansea Bay

Gareth Edwards
Welsh Rugby Union player
Born near Port Talbot, West Glamorgan
1947

Painted houses line the seafront at Tenby.

TENBY

PEMBROKE

St David's Cathedral

Carmarthen Bay

Puffins and seals live on Skomer Island.

Skomer Island

Tanni Grey-Thompson
Athlete and politician
Born in Cardiff, South Glamorgan
1969

3 Offa's Dyke is a massive bank and ditch earthworks along the Wales–England border. It was constructed in the 8th century for the English King Offa of Mercia.

4 There were once many coal mines in the Rhondda Valley. Today, the **Rhondda Heritage Park** commemorates the area's mining history.

Southern Scotland

Coll

TOBERMORY

Tiree

INNER HEBRIDES

Mull

McCaig's Tower stands above Oban.

Duart Castle

Iona

OBAN

Corryvreckan Whirlpool

Red deer

1 Opened in 1965, **Cruachan** is a hydroelectric power station located near Loch Awe. There's a visitor centre nearby.

Sea eagle

Colonsay

ARGYLL

Whisky distillery

Jura

Otter

Islay

TARBERT

Purple saxifrage flowers

Golden eagle

Oysters

Burns Night celebrates the birth of Robert Burns on 25th January. A haggis is ceremoniously piped in before guests sit down to a supper of haggis and whisky and listen to readings of his poetry.

Robert Burns
Poet
Born near Ayr, Strathclyde
1759-1796

Mull of Kintyre foghorn

Arr

Rajinder Singh
Chef and restaurateur
Born near Edinburgh
1971

White-beaked dolphin

North Channel

Mary Somerville
Scientist and writer
Born in Jedburgh, Borders
1780-1872
Somerville College in Oxford is named after her.

2 The **Falkirk Wheel** is a rotating boat lift that moves boats between the Forth & Clyde Canal and the Union Canal.

A busy ferry service runs between Stranraer and Belfast.

William Wallace
Born in Elderslie, near Glasgow
1270-1305

Wallace was one of the main leaders of the Wars of Independence against the English. He was later captured and executed in London.

The Wallace Monument at Stirling was built in 1869 to commemorate William Wallace.

The Old Course at St Andrews is the oldest golf course in the world.

Haddock

Gannet

For about 400 years, families of raiders known as the Border Reivers terrorised the Scotland-England border.

Kelpies sculptures

CENTRAL

Loch Lomond and the Trossachs National Park

STIRLING

FIFE

ST ANDREWS

Firth of Forth

Forth Bridge

Discover more about Glasgow on page 31.

DUNOON

FALKIRK

②

EDINBURGH

LOTHIAN

You can find out more about Edinburgh on page 26.

St Abb's Head

Lammermuir Hills

ELDERSLIE   GLASGOW

Riverside Museum, Glasgow

Some flights for Glasgow use Prestwick Airport.

STRATHCLYDE

The Honours of Scotland, or Crown Jewels, are kept in Edinburgh Castle.

③

Wanlockhead Lead Mining Museum

JEDBURGH

BORDERS

The ruins of Jedburgh Abbey date from the 12th century.

PRESTWICK

Firth of Clyde

AYR

GIRVAN

Dark Sky Observatory

Drumlanrig Castle is a magnificent fairytale castle.

The Devil's Porridge Museum tells the story of a First World War munitions factory.

DUMFRIES

Shortbread is a traditional Scottish biscuit.

Barn owl

Red squirrel

The Galloway Forest is the largest forest in Britain.

DUMFRIES & GALLOWAY

STRANRAER

WHITHORN   Solway Firth

Ancient stone cross at Whithorn

3 You can visit **Abbotsford** – the home of Walter Scott (1771-1832), one of Scotland's most famous writers.

Northern Scotland

Madainn mhath (pronounced 'mahteen vah') means 'Good morning'.

In many parts of Scotland, especially in the north and on the islands, the ancient Scottish Gaelic language is spoken.

ATLANTIC OCEAN

1 A huge, long-necked sea creature known as the **Loch Ness Monster**, or 'Nessie', is said to inhabit Loch Ness. Over many centuries, people have claimed to have seen it, but it has never been proved to exist.

2 **Skara Brae** is a Stone Age village over 5,000 years old. Visitors can see inside the rooms of houses.

3 **Up Helly Aa** is a fire festival held in the Shetland Islands in mid-winter. A procession of people carrying flaming torches throw them onto a replica of a wooden Viking longship.

4 You can catch a steam train that crosses the spectacular **Glenfinnan Viaduct**.

The national dress of Scotland is the **kilt**, made of wool tartan material. Each **Scottish clan** (family) has a tartan with its own patterns and colours.

Carved from walrus ivory nearly 1,000 years ago, these **chess pieces** were discovered on Lewis in 1831.

Lewis chessmen

Lewis

STORNOWAY

The Minch

Gannets

St Kilda

OUTER HEBRIDES

Harris

North Uist

Killer whale

South Uist

INNER HEBRIDES

Dunvegan Castle

PORTREE

Skye

Skye Br

Barra

Salmon

Rum

MALLAIG

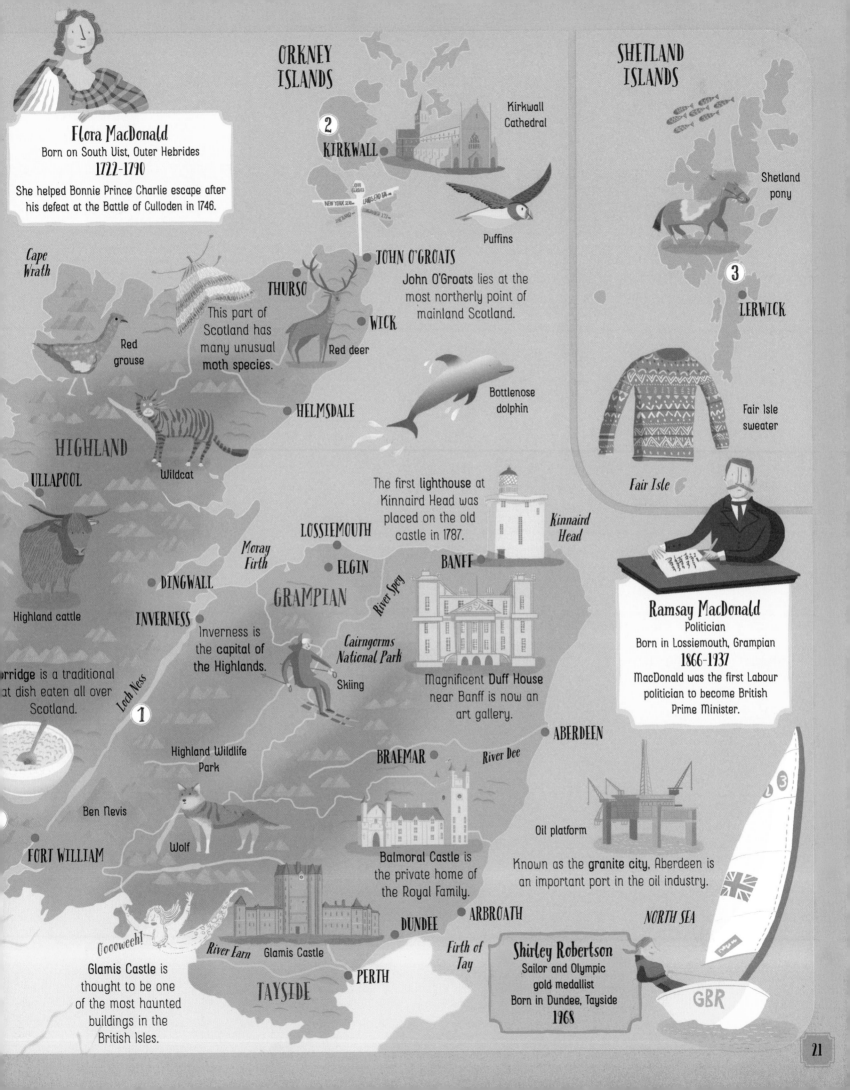

Flora MacDonald
Born on South Uist, Outer Hebrides
1722-1790
She helped Bonnie Prince Charlie escape after his defeat at the Battle of Culloden in 1746.

ORKNEY ISLANDS

SHETLAND ISLANDS

Kirkwall Cathedral

② KIRKWALL

Puffins

Shetland pony

JOHN O'GROATS
John O'Groats lies at the most northerly point of mainland Scotland.

③

LERWICK

Cape Wrath

THURSO
This part of Scotland has many unusual moth species.

WICK

Red deer

Red grouse

HELMSDALE

Bottlenose dolphin

Fair Isle sweater

HIGHLAND

 ULLAPOOL

Wildcat

Fair Isle

Highland cattle

The first lighthouse at Kinnaird Head was placed on the old castle in 1787.

Kinnaird Head

LOSSIEMOUTH

Moray Firth

DINGWALL

ELGIN

BANFF

GRAMPIAN

River Spey

Ramsay MacDonald
Politician
Born in Lossiemouth, Grampian
1866-1937
MacDonald was the first Labour politician to become British Prime Minister.

INVERNESS
Inverness is the capital of the Highlands.

Cairngorms National Park

Skiing

orridge is a traditional at dish eaten all over Scotland.

Loch Ness

①

Magnificent Duff House near Banff is now an art gallery.

ABERDEEN

Highland Wildlife Park

BRAEMAR

River Dee

Ben Nevis

Wolf

Oil platform

FORT WILLIAM

Balmoral Castle is the private home of the Royal Family.

Known as the granite city, Aberdeen is an important port in the oil industry.

Oooooeeh!

River Earn

Glamis Castle

DUNDEE

ARBROATH

NORTH SEA

Shirley Robertson
Sailor and Olympic gold medallist
Born in Dundee, Tayside
1968

Glamis Castle is thought to be one of the most haunted buildings in the British Isles.

TAYSIDE

PERTH

Firth of Tay

GBR

Ireland

"How sweetly lies old Ireland
Emerald green beyond the foam
Awakening sweet memories
Calling the heart back home."

An old Irish blessing

George Best
Footballer
Born in Belfast
1946–2005

Van Morrison
Singer and songwriter
Born in Belfast
1945

Golden eagle

Meadow pipit

Skylark

MAYO

Ballycroy National Park

SLIGO

KNOCK

The Knock Shrine is an important religious site.

Traditional thatched cottages at Glencolmcille Folk Village

Pottery has been made at Belleek since 1857.

DONEGAL

Malin Head

Fanad Head lighthouse

Glenveagh National Park

DONEGAL

BELLEEK

Lough Erne

ENNISKILLEN

FERMANAGH

LEITRIM

River Shannon

LONGFORD

ROSCOMMO

CAVAN

MONAGHAN

Newgrange is a huge prehistoric ceremonial site built over 5,000 years ago.

MEATH

WESTMEATH

DROGHEDA

LOUTH

DUNDALK

ARMAGH

ARMAGH

Soda farls are a delicious type of bread made in Northern Ireland.

TYRONE

River Blackwater

LONDONDERRY/
DERRY

LONDONDERRY

PORTSTEWART

River Bann

ANTRIM

3

Antrim Coast Road

1

BALLYMENA

Lough Neagh

BELFAST

2

DOWN

Mourne Mountains

NORTHERN IRELAND

REPUBLIC OF IRELAND

Find out more about Belfast on page 29.

ATLANTIC OCEAN

Spoonbill

Connemara

1 The Antrim Coast Road forms part of a coastal route around Northern Ireland. Near Portstewart, you'll pass the ruins of Dunluce Castle above the cliffs.

2 The Discovery Centre is a bird-watching and nature reserve on Lough Neagh, the largest lake in the British Isles.

3 The Giant's Causeway is a natural wonder formed 50 million years ago.

London

Founded by the Romans nearly 2,000 years ago, London is the capital of the United Kingdom and one of the largest, most exciting cities in the world.

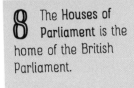

8 The **Houses of Parliament** is the home of the British Parliament.

9 Completed in 1711, **St Paul's Cathedral** is one of the largest cathedrals in the world.

Zadie Smith
Author
Born in London
1975

MUSEUMS OF LONDON

1 Discover fossils and dinosaurs dating back millions of years at the **Natural History Museum**.

2 In the **Science Museum** you can find out about science and technology of the past, present and future.

3 The **Victoria & Albert Museum** contains one of the world's largest collections of decorative arts.

4 With 8 million objects covering thousands of years, the **British Museum** is one of the world's most famous museums.

5 The **Imperial War Museum** has planes, tanks and other vehicles from the First and Second World Wars.

6 **Oxford Street** is one of the busiest shopping streets in the world.

7 At **St Pancras Station**, you can catch a speedy Eurostar train to mainland Europe.

Underground trains carry 1.35 billion people around London every year.

10 The **Tower of London** was built over 900 years ago and is home to the Crown Jewels.

11 **Buckingham Palace** is the London home of the Queen.

ROYAL PARKS

Learie Constantine
Cricketer, lawyer and politician
Played cricket at Lord's
1901–1971

Howzat!

13
The Regent's Park

Lord's Cricket Ground

14 Speakers' Corner

Marble Arch

Hyde Park

Kensington Gardens

18
1 **2** **3**

Cromwell Road

Fulham Road

Battersea Power Station

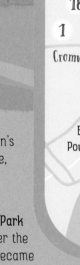

Battersea Park

12 Once a royal deer park beside the River Thames, **Greenwich Park** contains the Queen's House, the Old Royal Naval College, museums and an observatory.

13 **The Regent's Park** is named after the Prince Regent, who became King George IV in 1820.

LONDON ZOO

The park contains ornamental gardens, a lake and a famous zoo with giraffes, penguins and lots of other animals.

14 Held over two days every August, **Notting Hill Carnival** is led by members of the British West Indian community. It is one of the world's biggest street festivals. Thousands dress in bright costumes and play music.

15 **Queen Elizabeth Olympic Park** is a sporting venue in east London, built for the 2012 Summer Olympics and Paralympics. It's now used as a sports complex, with stadiums and swimming pools, and is surrounded by a landscaped park with a river and gardens.

Upper Street

7 Euston Road

The **Gherkin** is the nickname of an office building at 30, St Mary Axe.

Marylebone Road

Completed in 2012, **The Shard** is the tallest building in London.

Red **telephone boxes** are dotted around London.

4

Oxford Street

6

Theobald's Road

Nelson's Column

17

9

Whitechapel Road

Commercial Road

David Attenborough
Naturalist and broadcaster
Born in London
1926

16

20

Tate Modern

10

The Highway

Tower Bridge

River Thames

19

11

Westminster Abbey

8

The London Eye

New Kent Road

5

An area called **Elephant and Castle** is said to get its name from Henry VIII's first wife, the Infanta of Castile and Aragon.

People have been buying food at **Borough Market** since at least 1276.

One of the main financial districts of the world, **Canary Wharf** contains some of the tallest buildings in Europe.

Tate Britain

Vauxhall Bridge

River Thames

Nine Elms Lane

12

MUSIC AND THEATRE

16 The **West End** is the main entertainment area of London – full of theatres, cinemas, clubs, cafés and restaurants.

18 Opened in 1871, the **Royal Albert Hall** is one of the most famous concert halls in the world.

19 Built to celebrate the start of the third millennium in 2000, **The Dome** is now used as an entertainment venue.

Mica Paris
Singer and actor
Born in London
1969

17 The **Royal Opera House** is one of the world's great opera houses.

20 The **Globe Theatre** is an exact copy of a theatre from the time of William Shakespeare, 400 years ago.

Edinburgh
Capital of Scotland

This spectacular city is built on seven hills. It's the second most visited city in Britain, after London, and home to the world-famous Edinburgh International Festival.

Robert Louis Stevenson
Novelist and travel writer
Born in Edinburgh
1850-1894

In this description from his story, *The Strange Case of Dr Jekyll and Mr Hyde*, Robert Louis Stevenson was inspired by Edinburgh's Old Town.

> "... the whole city leads a double existence... it is half alive and half a monumental marble."

Marie Stopes
Palaeobotanist and writer
Born in Edinburgh
1880-1958

HMY Britannia was the royal yacht of Queen Elizabeth II. It sailed over 160,000km (100,000 miles) around the world, and is now moored at Leith, north of the city.

Members of the British Royal Family stay in the **Palace of Holyroodhouse** during official visits to Scotland.

Politicians meet in the **Scottish Parliament Building** to discuss important matters and make new laws.

Salisbury Crags

Edinburgh is nicknamed 'Auld Reekie', which is the Scots for 'Old Smoky'. Thick smoke filled the alleyways of the Old Town during medieval times.

One of Edinburgh's hills is called Arthur's Seat. It was formed by a volcano that was last active 350 million years ago.

Holyrood Road

WHEEOOOAAARR!

You can hear **street musicians** playing Highland bagpipes.

Edinburgh's Old Town is the medieval part of the city. It's full of twisting alleyways, narrow vaults and hidden underground passages. The central streets are called the Royal Mile.

The Royal Mile

Pleasance

THE EDINBURGH FESTIVAL!

Nicolson Street

North Bridge

Princes Street

St Giles Cathedral

Greyfriars Bobby is a statue commemorating a Skye terrier that spent 14 years guarding his master's grave, until his own death in 1872.

Every August, around a million visitors flock to the city to take part in the Edinburgh International Festival, which celebrates art, science and culture.

Author J. K. Rowling began writing the first *Harry Potter* book in this small café in the Old Town.

the elephant house

The Mound

Grassmarket

Perched high on Castle Rock, Edinburgh Castle is a towering fortress dating from the 12th century.

BOOM!

Mons Meg is one of the largest medieval cannons in the world. Visitors can see it at Edinburgh Castle.

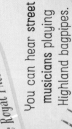

Cardiff
Capital of Wales

From a glitzy waterfront to ancient castle ruins, Cardiff is a city of old and new. It's been the capital of Wales since 1955.

Just to the north of Cardiff is **Castell Coch** – a medieval castle which was updated during the 19th century. It now looks like a fantasy castle, with pointed towers and a drawbridge.

2 Politicians meet in the **Senedd** to make new laws.

3 The public gardens of **Cathays Park** are surrounded by grand stone buildings put up in the early 20th century.

Some of the interior decorations

Many of the rooms inside the castle are decorated with ornate furniture and spectacular painted walls.

8 **Cardiff Bay Wetlands Reserve** is a reedy marshland in Cardiff Bay. It's a haven for birds and other water-loving creatures.

1 **National Museum Cardiff** is packed full of interesting exhibits, from mammoths to paintings by Monet.

Shirley Bassey
Singer
Born in Cardiff
1937

4 **Cardiff Castle** is part Roman fort, part Norman keep and part Victorian manor.

7 **The Coal Exchange** is a stately building once used as the meeting place for coal traders and ship owners.

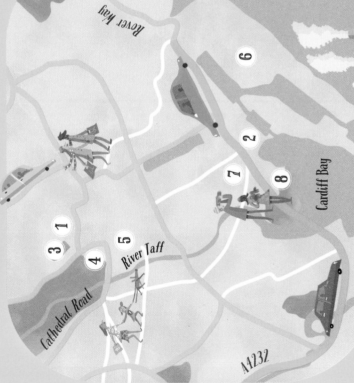

Rover Bay

River Taff

Cathedral Road

A4232

Cardiff Bay

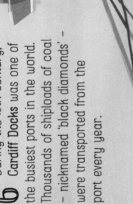

6 During the 19th century, **Cardiff Docks** was one of the busiest ports in the world. Thousands of shiploads of coal – nicknamed 'black diamonds' – were transported from the port every year.

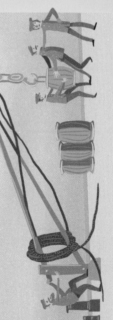

Gareth Bale
Footballer
Born in Cardiff
1989

If you're lucky, you'll spot a pair of **Peregrine falcons** nesting on Cardiff's City Hall.

5 The **Principality Stadium** is a 74,500-seat stadium with a sliding roof that opens and shuts. It hosts rugby matches, concerts and other big events.

Dublin
Capital of the Republic of Ireland

First settled by Vikings from Scandinavia in the 10th century, Dublin is a city that's steeped in history. It's named after 'Dubh Linn', a muddy tidal pool that once lay near the River Liffey.

James Joyce   Maeve Binchy   Elizabeth Bowen   Samuel Beckett

"...if I can get to the heart of Dublin I can get to the heart of all the cities of the world..."

James Joyce, quoted in *From the Old Waterford House* by Arthur Power

A writer's city

Dublin is the birthplace of many famous writers, from Samuel Beckett and William Butler Yeats to Elizabeth Bowen and Maeve Binchy. James Joyce's well-known works, *The Dubliners* and *Ulysses*, are set in and around Dublin.

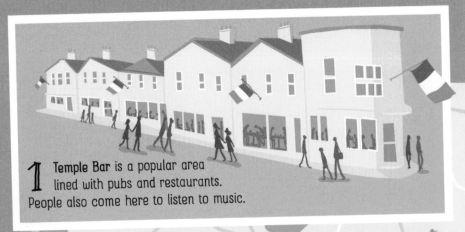

1 Temple Bar is a popular area lined with pubs and restaurants. People also come here to listen to music.

Royal Canal

Dorset Street

North Circular

The **Spire of Dublin** is a huge needle-like sculpture that beams light into the city's night sky.

Parnell Street

O'Connell Street

Samuel Beckett Bridge

Phoenix Park

The **Four Courts** is Ireland's main law courts building.

River Liffey

1

2

Museum of Modern Art

Kilmainham

Christ Church Cathedral is over 1,000 years old. It's famous for its huge underground crypt and ornate floor tiles.

Patterned floor tiles

Ha'penny Bridge

Dublin Castle was built by English King John in 1204. It was originally used to protect the King's treasure.

Merrion Square is a park surrounded by elegant 18th-century houses. Ever since the square was completed, this has been a very fashionable area.

Pearse Street

"In Dublin's fair city, where the girls are so pretty, I first set my eyes on sweet Molly Malone..."

Lyrics from *Cockles and Mussels*, a traditional song set in Dublin

2 Founded by Elizabeth I in 1592, Trinity College is a world-famous university.

Inside Trinity College Library, visitors can see the **Book of Kells**, a magnificent manuscript dating back to the year 800.

Belfast
Capital of Northern Ireland

Sitting on the banks of the River Lagan and surrounded by hills, Belfast is the largest city and port in Northern Ireland.

1 In the 19th and 20th centuries, Belfast was one of the greatest ship-building cities in the world. Huge yellow cranes known as **Samson and Goliath** still dominate the north east area of the city.

High above the city sits **Belfast Castle**, which was built in 1870. Legend has it that if a white cat lives there the castle residents will have good fortune.

2 In the **Ulster Museum** visitors can see gold coins from the Spanish Armada, wrecked off the coast of Northern Ireland in 1588.

3 Opened in 1828, the **Botanic Gardens** have splendid glasshouses with exotic plants.

Once the world's largest **linen producer**, Belfast was nicknamed 'Linenopolis'. The linen was woven in huge mills and shipped all over the world.

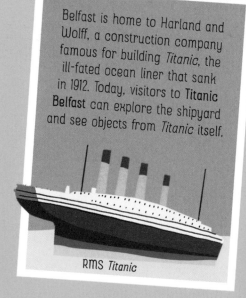
Belfast is home to Harland and Wolff, a construction company famous for building *Titanic*, the ill-fated ocean liner that sank in 1912. Today, visitors to *Titanic* Belfast can explore the shipyard and see objects from *Titanic* itself.

RMS *Titanic*

C.S. Lewis
Author
Born near Belfast
1878-1963

Albert Memorial Clock

St Anne's Cathedral

Queen's Bridge

Titanic Belfast **1**

Concerts and plays take place in the **Waterfront Hall.**

Grand Opera House

City Hall was built in 1906. It's a huge stone building, where important council meetings are held.

Albert Bridge

River Lagan

Jocelyn Bell Burnell
Astrophysicist
Born near Belfast
1943
Credited with discovering the first radio pulsars in 1967

Westlink

Spanish canon in the Ulster Museum

Donegall Road

Lisburn Road

University Road

Ormeau Road

3 **2** **Queen's University** was opened in 1849 and is one of the United Kingdom's leading universities.

International rugby matches are held beneath the floodlights of the **Kingspan Stadium.**

Manchester

The Romans built a fort here called Mancunium in the year 79, and by the Middle Ages, Manchester had developed into a prosperous town. From the early 19th century it quickly grew into an enormous city and one of Britain's main industrial areas.

"Manchester... the belly and guts of the Nation."

From *The Road to Wigan Pier* by George Orwell

The football stadium at **Old Trafford**, to the south of the city, is home to Manchester United Football Club.

Electric **trams** were first used in 1901, but the present system dates from 1992.

The **Arndale Centre** is one of Britain's largest shopping centres.

The **Northern Quarter** is a busy area of the city lined with bars, cafés and music shops.

Swan Street

Oldham Road

Deansgate

River Irwell

The **John Rylands Library**, opened in 1900, contains a fabulous collection of books and manuscripts.

Completed in 1877, the **Town Hall** is one of England's grandest public buildings.

Piccadilly Gardens

Piccadilly

You can visit a reconstruction of one of the Roman gateways at the **Mancunium Roman Fort**.

Beetham Tower is a 47-storey tower block containing offices, a hotel and apartments.

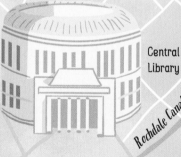

Central Library

Rochdale Canal

Trains run into **Piccadilly Station**, in the heart of the city.

ROVERS RETURN INN

At **Media City**, to the west of the city, you can take a tour of the studio set of *Coronation Street*, Britain's longest running soap opera.

Emmeline Pankhurst
Political activist
Born in Moss Side, Manchester
1855–1928

Pankhurst was leader of the British suffragette movement which helped women win the right to vote.

Glasgow

Scotland's largest city, in the Middle Ages Glasgow grew from a small settlement on the River Clyde into a great seaport. During the 19th century, the city became one of the world's main places for shipbuilding, engineering and textiles.

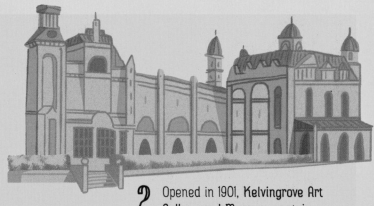

2 Opened in 1901, **Kelvingrove Art Gallery and Museum** contains one of the finest collections of armour in the world.

1 No longer used, the **Finnieston Crane** once lifted heavy cargo onto ships.

3 Housed in a building dating from 1778, the **Gallery of Modern Art** contains paintings and sculptures. Over the portico is a mosaic by artist Niki de Saint Phalle.

The **Botanic Gardens** have been in their present location in the north of the city since 1842. They contain a number of glasshouses for exotic plants, the most famous being the **Kibble Palace**.

Carol Ann Duffy
Poet Laureate
Born in Glasgow
1926

Glasgow is Britain's **curry capital**, with half the population eating a curry at least once a week.

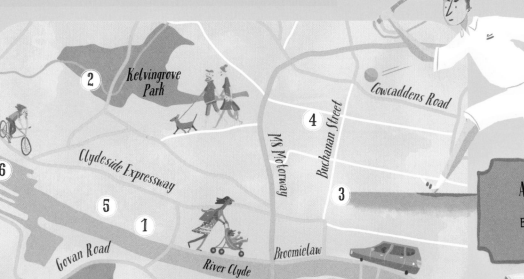

Andy Murray
Tennis player
Born in Glasgow
1987

5 The **Armadillo** auditorium holds sports events, concerts and plays.

Charles Rennie Mackintosh
Architect, designer and artist
Born in Glasgow
1868-1928

4 One of the most famous buildings of the 20th century, the **School of Art** was designed by Charles Rennie Mackintosh.

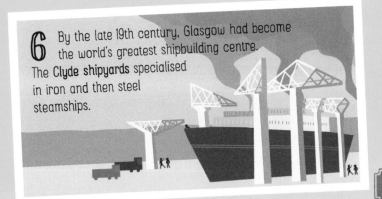

6 By the late 19th century, Glasgow had become the world's greatest shipbuilding centre. The **Clyde shipyards** specialised in iron and then steel steamships.